The Black *Pen*

LaDonna Letitia

GoPublish
Delray Beach, Florida

THE BLACK PEN
Copyright © 2021 by LaDonna Letitia

All rights reserved.

Cover art by Edward J Stinson III

No part of this book may be reproduced or transmitted in any form or by any means, electronic or mechanical, including photocopying, recording, or by any information storage and retrieval system, without permission in writing from the copyright owner.

Published by GoPublish, Delray Beach, Florida.

GoPublish
14280 Military Trail, #7501
Delray Beach, Florida 33482

www.VisualAdjectives.com
info@VisAdj.com

Library of Congress Control Number: 2021923594

ISBN-13: 978-1-941901-43-4 (EBook)
          978-1-941901-42-7 (trade paperback)
ISBN-10: 1-941901-42-5 (trade paperback)

First American Paperback Edition: October 2021

I dedicate this, my first published work, to my son Corban…
And to all the other black lives who matter.

Introduction

Love and Light to you!
I'm LaDonna. It's so wonderful to meet you
and share space with you.

Poetry is such a sacred space, dontcha think?
I've been writing poetry since I was a little girl. I was raised
by my mother, an English teacher. She had me reading
Maya Angelou in the third grade, so believe me when I say,
it's in my blood.

Another unavoidable truth within, is my blackness. I am a
black woman born and raised in America. I have fallen in
love, black. I have struggled, black. I have grown up, black.
This book of poems is the representation of that.

Acknowledgments

I'd like to thank my mommy momster, for being the awesome black woman she is; Ever hard, ever kind, everlastingly ever herself. She is the rock who represents the midnight tears of black single mothers worldwide who hide their pain and struggle from their offspring. You make it look easy mommy.

Thank you to my twin flame, Harrison G., you are such an exceptional human being, my love. I am because you are, you are because I am.

Special thanks to my muse, Darius D. You are the match that lights the flames of creativity in all whom have the pleasure of knowing you.

Thank you to Edward S. aka Tre, for the cover art, your artistry is KING.

Thank you to my sistar and best friend Nyia B. for walking with me on every path since the day we met. Your love and support is unmatched.

Thank you to my brother, lover, homie Shawn; my master teacher... look at us, doing what we always said we would.

Thank you to my family (Auntie Bev; My wisdom, Auntie Val; My truth, Kim; My aspiration, Conrad & Avery; Our dreams fulfilled), for being exactly who you are.

Demario P, I thank you for being my feedback and my writing partna since way back when. You're next, my friend.

Thank you Domonique B... aka "Poe" for your inspiration. The moment you published your first book, I knew I could and would publish too, and you have supported me every step of the way.

Momma Sabira, thank you for your spirit, I give "Two Young Girls" to you and Jafar.

Ashely B., thank you for your strength and creativity, I give "Step Queen, Step", to you. Pat & Angie... I miss him too. I give "Sha" to you.

Thank you to my Soul Tribe (T'fawnia C, Shannon G, Carrie J and Brandie M) for pouring into me over the years and pushing me to be my highest self.

Roney P, thanks for the lessons over the years. I Love me more because of them.

Slim P, thanks for always having my back.
Jonathan M, thanks for always believing in me.

Thank you to Bridges & Pathways To Prosperity, Inc. in Boynton for teaching me self- love and discipline K. Bush and T.Hails... you raise the standard for black excellence.

Thank you to my family at The Spady Cultural Heritage Museum, Charlene F. and Sharon B, for teaching me to unapologetically love and honor my blackness.

And to so many others (family, friends, exes, foes, associates, co-workers and mentors), I thank you for every word of encouragement and every listening ear... for the breaking, the growing, the inspiration and lessons... I love you. You matter to me.

The Black *Pen*

Table of Contents

BLACK STRIFE
- Write The Truth 14
- Dear America 16
- Cousin Kim Pt 1 18
- HIS_Story 22
- Sha 24
- SONshine Dreams 28
- Two Young Girls 30
- When The World Falls Down 34
- Black Berries 36

BLACK FAITH
- Sunday Morning Hats 40
- Amen 42
- Oya 44
- Oshun 46
- Shango 48
- God 52
- Holy Water 56

BLACK LOVE
- Worship 60
- Hot Cocoa 62
- Another Chocolate Kiss 64
- Linger Longer 66
- Where Love Walks 68
- The Space We Share 70
- Ignite Me 74
- Intimacy 78
- Tall, Dark, and Delicious 80

BLACK LIFE
- Soft Spaces 84
- Air 86
- Pride 90
- In Love With Being Black 92
- Step Queen, Step 96
- Bull City Bad 98
- The Yard 102
- Hair Washing Day 106
- More (an ode to black women) 110
- The Hungry 114
- All Hail The Black Pen 118

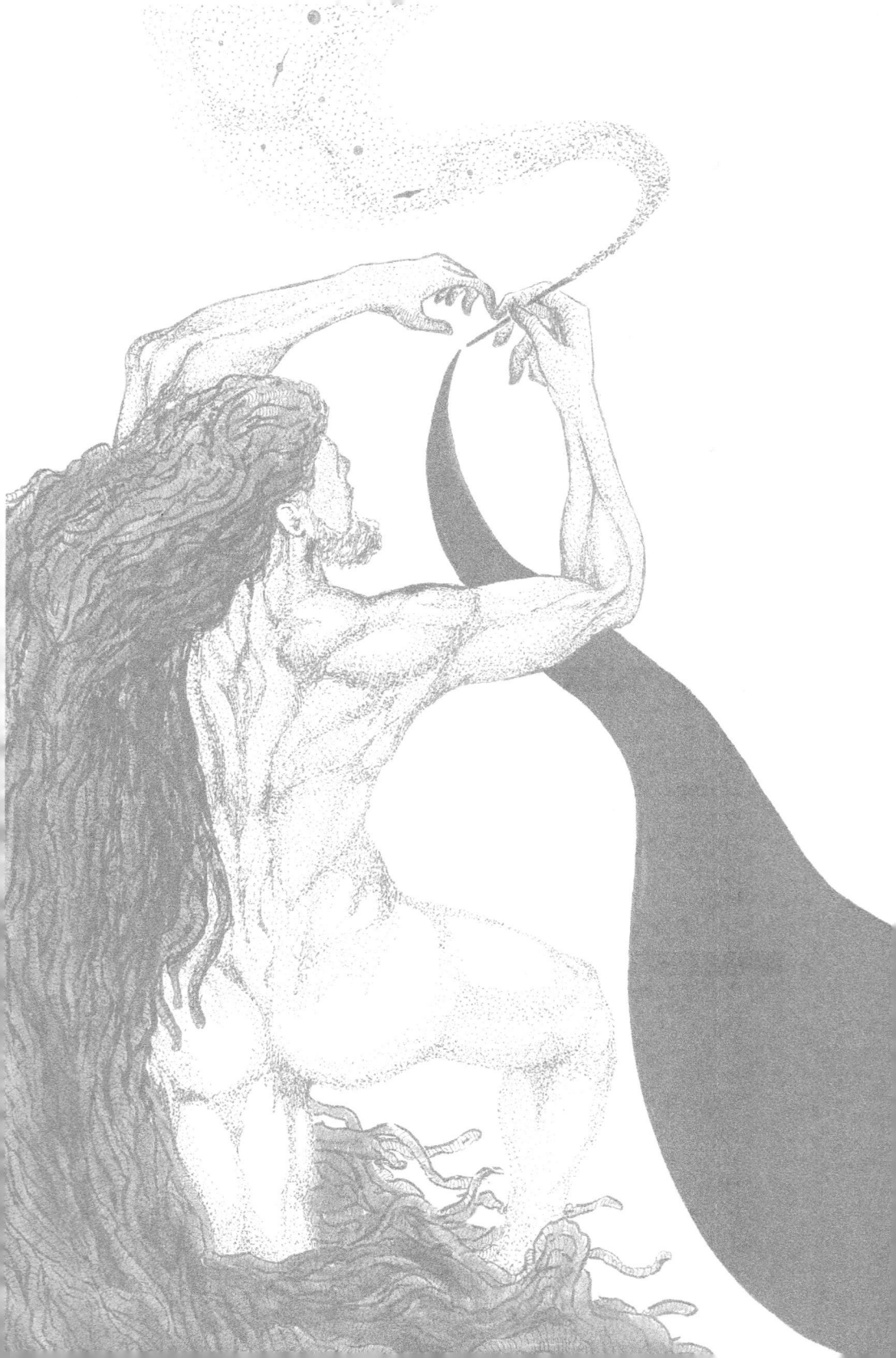

Black

Strife

Write the Truth

THE BLACK PEN

Never asked a poet to write me a poem.

Nah, I just need something to write my pain on.

No lollipops, no gumdrops, no glitter, no love song

Instead, write out my mirror, reflect me my wrongs.

Never asked a poet to write me a smile.

I'm too afraid to fake it. Too scared and too wild.

Don't give me false hopes with your paper and pen.

Don't glorify my glory with the spotlight on my wins.

No, dearest poet, write me a straight line

Drawn across my forehead, the hardships of time

Write me a war song, yes! Sing me a blues

Save the lies for the lost, for the me's, write the truth.

Dear America

THE BLACK PEN

My dearest America,

Do you know how to love someone like me?

Someone seemingly so bound, who's mind remains free?

Tell me, America, do you love at all?

In God you trust right? Yet, for printed trees you fall.

You keep flapping your golden wings, trying to fulfill fleeting dreams

Telling us about the hope here, "trust in me" you say "believe"

But, my dearest America, dost thou find us so naïve?

Trust in who? You? The warden of black kings?

You don't hate me because my skin looks like cocoa puffs...

Nor because my hair is knotted and calloused feet rough

But simply because I'm here and I CAN BREATHE

You hate that I won't submit, silently I take a knee.

I kneel always for justice and I stand against your war

I grant you my wisdom, all the knowledge lost before

You treat us like chained dogs; your red, white and blues leashed

The privilege of your brownstones built on breathtaking black dreams.

Dear America, my dear, has thou watered thine own roots?

I fear not, Lady Liberty, for thy has always been untrue.

Yet still, I love you.

Cousin Kim pt. 1

THE BLACK PEN

She was the prettier girl

When we were growing up

Full lips, "good hair" and lighter skin

Tall, slender and a big butt

I was just the shadow

The dark one who tagged along

I would've killed to have her looks

And to feel like I belonged.

But I was more like cousin Troi

Poor, black and too skinny

Bony legs with a toothy smile

Only cute when I was grinning.

I used to wear long-sleeved shirts

In the hot ass summer heat

Sweating myself to misery

But not getting darker you see.

When cousin Kim was tanned

She went from almond to golden roast

I went from black to blacker than that

But no one yearns for burnt toast.

The boys would always see her first

They'd call her beautiful

I always got the left-over smiles

Last minute "hi's" and "hello's"

Man, I love my cousin Kim

Wanted to be like her you see

But as time went on "dark" was trending

And the pretty girl was me

That was a crazy switch up

Melanin: the thing to have

For so long we were taught light is right

And dark is ugly... bad.

THE BLACK PEN

But this ain't even bout cousin Kim

But the way the world saw us both

Two black girls who were never told

That all shades of black are beautiful.

HIS_Story

THE BLACK PEN

Chains 'round my feet keep rubbing wrong
Praying to white paintings, singing Negro songs
They be lost souls who done lost their old ways
'cus massah say "once you be slave, you always be slave"

It's hard to run with these things weighing me down
Hard to work hard, stones won't let me drown
Cotton pickin, cane cuttin, paper pushin; all the same
Red, white and blue dreams to sleep to, they won't say our names

But momma told me that I was born free
Dressing me up for Jesus, Sundays let freedom sing
"Praise the Lord! Praise the Lord! My baby is saved!"
But I hear whispers "once you be slave you always be slave"

They tell me find a good man, God-fearing and true
Make sure he knows the Lord God, and he'll be good to you
Saw Pastor Mitchell strike his wife, they say 'cus she'a slut
But I s'posed to stay out it, head down, eyes and mouth shut.

Rope 'round my throat keep choking me, words I aint 'llowed to say
Yes'am, No'am, 's'all that break loose, no thoughts of my own "just pray"
Hard to be loud with a hand on yo mouth, "be a good girl now" he say
Momma knows but have no control cus once you be slave you always be slave.

Daddy gone, he done left us here. Too bound to even care
They took his crown and shot him down, blood stains in his underwear
Give us us free, give us us tongues, Give us us gods back
History will tell that it's better now, 't'aint; we still chained, we still black.

Sha

THE BLACK PEN

13, thinks

It feels, it breathes

13, we were, we are...

Wishing on 13 black stars

13 days after

Love, prayed

But 13 preyed on love

Lucky for me,

13 is my birthday.

He thought I was a dream

Even on my worst day

When my heart bled, 07

She swam her way to Heaven

13 days in Solitude

Sha and me

Us 2, 24/7

Lost him once

2013, found

True story, I swear

That's when the boy,

The man was recrowned

But Sha had many Queens

Many thrones

Many black beds

Probably 13 of us

26 tears shed.

Sha had 13 sorrows

Most of them inside

Thought himself unworthy

Wanted to provide, but,

Never settled down

Never settled in

13 disappointments

Only wanted 1 win

THE BLACK PEN

Never said goodbye

We always left with hello

Lived in 13 shades of black

But loved my yellow

Funny the track he chose

Beautiful girl, suicidal

13 years after that

And those 13s hit like a tidal

He left behind himself

In the eyes of growing seed,

Those other 12 girls,

Those unfilled dreams,

1 brotha

Lucky 13

And unlucky, me.

May he rest in peace.

SONShine Dreams

THE BLACK PEN

Little baby boy, my sweet little one
Welcome to planet Earth
The Heavens rejoice at the sound of your cry
This, the grand day of your birth.
Wish I could keep you in my arms forever
Wish you could always be mine
But some day you'll be the greatest in all the land
A master teacher, a powerful black man in time.

Little baby boy, sweet little one
May your childhood be pure and true
Run free, my sweet boy, wild and loud in paved pastures
Black rivers and skies, blue.
Wish I could tell you, my little black boy
That life will never beat you down
Wish I could protect you from the struggles to come
The hardships of your skin painted brown.

Little baby boy, my sweet little one
Eyes bright and filled with dreams
Don't run my sweet boy, don't resist, don't speak
They are not at all what they seem.
Wish I could hold your hand that day
That is surely to someday come
I hope you remember where your hands should be
And I pray that you make it home.

Little baby boy, sweet little one
Our wombs have cried many tears
They've sworn with their lives to protect us all
Yet, now we live our greatest of fears.
I wish I could hold you one last time
Kiss your sweet face beneath full moons
Rest well black boy, for your name never dies
Just like all the black dreamers gone too soon.

Two Young Girls

THE BLACK PEN

We were two black girls

Growing and learning

Talking about slashing

And crying… always crying

When they broke our hearts again.

We were dancers

Pointing our toes

Moving our hips

Laughing at our teachers

Who thought they knew better

They didn't know any better.

We were rebels.

They told us to keep it down

So we screamed "Darling Nikki" louder

And other loud things.

High heels and kicks

TLC and lunch cliques

We were tight.

As tight as we could be.

We liked the same boys

The same boys liked us back

Didn't bother us though

We didn't fuss

We left that to the silly girls

Snickering and bickering

We were above that.

We had Purple Rain

We had Graffiti Bridge

We had step team "you know"!

We had Mary... your Allah, my Jesus

We share late nights at the Cantina

We rocked afros

Before kinks were trending

We had knots and braids

5'2" and slim thicks

Before the white house

Before we could concentrate

Before the eagles soared for us

Before Dream Girls and Bey Hives

Before dorm hot plates

And sloping hills of green

Before dance battles

Before magenta splatters

Were painted white...

We laughed

We grew

We fought together

We learned

And we broke down walls

And made weird normal

We were us.

We were black...

THE BLACK PEN

We were "sis" and "yes Queen"

Before the hashtags

From Badu and Ms. Hill to CeeLo

Beyonce, Ciara and Legend

We had us. We had we.

Two young girls...

Two young black girls

Growing and Glowing

Bless it be.

When The World Falls Down

THE BLACK PEN

What do you do when the world falls down
Smack dead on your head... like, the whole damned town?
Nothing feels right... Nothing is right...
You know how to swim right? But still, you drown.

Where do you go when you have no home
When you've been flipped upside down, roaming alone?
Struck by the past and trying to get back
Trying to break free from old chains, still you're owned.

How do you smile with the world on your back
Right between your shoulder blades tryin to carry all of that?
They say one thing but I know one thing...
Best balance that weight good or your back gonna crack.

Who do you pray to when your voice is broke
Scratchy and sore from the wail stuck in your throat
You wanna scream for help but screaming hurts like hell
So many words incarcerated trying to break free but you choke.

When do you know for sure that the world has gone cold?
Tick Tocks and broken clocks as time grows old
Back aches are crying, knees weak and dying
Waiting for the hands to change, keep waiting? Or fold?

What do you do when the world falls down
Childlike scraping knee caps on broken paved grounds
You keep pushing! That's what, lemons turn to lemonade
Grandmothers long gone awaiting your freedom when your reflection is brown.

Black Berries

THE BLACK PEN

She's a sweet one
Sweeter than most
You'd never even know
You'd never know her life
It has been difficult.
Lights go out now
Her smile shines through
1999 she stayed inside
The entire month of June
She wears all black
It lightens up her skin
Yellows make it glow too
Island mom, African dad
Grand from Trinidad
Spicy foods on holidays
Skin too dark to tan
All her friends are almonds
Paper bags and sugar browns
All her heroes love honey wheat
Red clays and apache towns
They compare her to campfires
Charcoal black and midnight skies
She aint the reflection of rolling clouds
To them, black shit, black flies
But the thing is she's a sweet one
She's actually sweeter than most
She stands out in a crowd
Not like coal or dog shit but
Blackberries in white snow.

Black

Faith

Sunday Morning Hats

THE BLACK PEN

First Sundays are always white

Big feathers and glittering gold

Second Sundays are navy blue

Pin striped, peacock in the fold.

Third Sundays is bloody red

A veil pulled to the right side.

Fourth Sundays are yellows and pinks

Sometimes greens preside.

Matching gloves, purse and shoes

Mother Shirley in the front left pew.

Greens been on since yesterday noon

Hot dogs for a dolla but only for the youth

First Sundays were always white

Big Feathers and glittering gold

Now we wear black and hunger cries

Sundays never felt so cold.

Amen

THE BLACK PEN

Woke up to the sound of papa prayin yonder
Momma clankin pots in the kitchen out back
Biscuits and gravy set on the table in the kitchen
Chickens drawing straws to see who's being set free
When night comes 'round, I s'pose we'll see
Sister went and found herself a workin fella
Momma beams so big and proud
Brother done got a job in town with Mr. Jankins
Never seen papa so down.
I puts on my new shiny black shoes
Yellow dress with flowers in the ruffles
Little white gloves and my hair pressed back
Ready for Sunday school.
Aunt Anne is still sick with fever, so the boys are here with us
Papa lookin mighty fine! Britches crisp and hair freshly cut
I grab butter from the coolin box
The house comes to a pause
We all sit down at the table and papa prays "God bless us all..."
Bless this food, bless the land
Bless his beautiful wife and kids
Heal aunt Anne, bless the boys
And them bad Williams boys in the neighborhood
Bless Pastor Miles
and his ailing wife, bless his mistress too
bless the cow, bless the ground bless the sun the moon and stars
bless our roof bless our faces bless our feet and our hands
bless the hens bring us sun and bring us rain
thank you for this food thank you Jesus,
together we say "amen"

THE BLACK PEN

She beckons death and sends it away

Calls forth life from frozen graves

She guards all tombs of fantasy

And the gateway to the resting places of dead things

Protector of all who have come and gone

Fighter for queens, all weak and all strong

Slicing through the turmoil on paths up ahead

A trail of fire trails her... fire, cowrie, pink and red

Drumming in her feet, as she stomps upon the lost

Bearing hips, full lips, and nursing breasts without cost

Hear her warrior cry, the roar of her undefeated

The earth gives way to her muddled steps energy un-depleted

She wades in murky waters that flow at her sultry voice

Great horns adorn her warrior crown, warring, her sacred choice

They never did mention her beauty before, too fearful of her fist

She is among the fairest still, her seduction your greatest bliss

All hail the mother goddess, who guards the dead and dying

She protects her own, maroon adorned her trail of blood un-drying.

Oshun

THE BLACK PEN

Come here lovers.
The sweetness of me beckons
Stare into me; my soul
My eyes... my thighs
Wade in me.
I command your senses
They are mine to do so
Love her, cherish her
Value him, honor him
Submit to me; your sensual guide
For I weave honey trails of sweet sex
And bitter wine...
For I weave honey trails of sweet sex
And bitter wine.
I open up her temple for her.
Giving her power over herself
Which gives her power over you.
She embodies my golden rays,
Sunlight, amber, copper and honey jars
She smells of me; baptismal pools,
Fresh baked pastries and fertility
Lay her down, lovers, in meadows beside me
Please her there, tease her there
Watch her blossom within me
I watch her dangle from eager fingers
And parched tongues
Hives filled with unspeakable desire
I gave her to herself
Now you give yourself to me.

Shango

THE BLACK PEN

Be my drummer

My medicine man

Be my warrior

My helping hand

Be my lover

My ecstasy

Be my king

My sovereignty

Be my storm

My lightning strike

Be my passion

My whispering might

Be my partner

My favorite song

Be my muse

My all night long

Be my blood

My menstrual flow

Be my teacher

My evening glow

Be my mischief

My warring youth

Be my rebel

My path for truth

Be my hope

My make believe

Be my earth

The God in me

Be my faith

My other half

Be my light

My Moses staff

Be my brother

My partner in life

My warrior, my drummer

My sky, my knife.

God

THE BLACK PEN

When I see you

I See God.

I see the created and the creator

I see Heaven and Earth...

I even see Hell.

I see love and passion and wrath

I see flowers sprouting and trees withering

I see lightning and rain

I see blue skies and sunshine

I see gold, I see life

I see you.

And when I see you, I see God.

I see father and mother

I see best friend, I see lover

I see all hurt

And all my healing

I see music and dancing

I see magic and I see light

I see laughter and tears

I see rainbows and wonder

I see you.

And when I see you,

I see God.

I see the shackled

I see the released

I see the impoverished

I see the wealthy

I see babies being born

I see grandparents being buried

I see ocean waves

I see seashells

Mountains, Valleys and deserts

THE BLACK PEN

I see the world in you...

I see you.

And when I do...

When I look at you...

When I hold you...

When I kiss you... when I dream of you...

When someday, I fall in love with you...

I'll be seeing God...

Falling in love with God

When I see you.

Amen, nah, AGod.

Holy Water

THE BLACK PEN

His mouth be like the Jordan

His spit be that anointing that cures blind eyes

He be lookin, and I be healin

He be talkin, and I be feelin

He be like the tide that carried slaves to freedom.

He be like Holy Water

Let him rain. Let him reign.

Black

Love

Worship

THE BLACK PEN

Bitter-sweet cocoa god, I bow my head at your waist

Mouth open...giving deep praise!

Crowning your head with my tongue, oh happy day!

Oh happy day! For this is the day that love has made

Baptizing me in the name of you, the father, you, the son, you,

The master teacher...

Preach preacher! Now I bow a little deeper

You are worthy, majestic one

Oh come by here, Lord King, cum.

Hot Cocoa

THE BLACK PEN

It's cold outside

Don't go home yet

Stay this night

Warm your thoughts by my fire

Your hands in my heat

Rest your thoughts upon my softness

Be comfortable, be free.

Lay your head on my pillow

Relax. Breathe. Inhale me.

It's cold outside...

And honestly, I'm a little thirsty, love

Quench me, warm me

Stay with me

Love me...

Melt.

Another Chocolate Kiss

THE BLACK PEN

If you want one… I don't mind

Feels real good, got me feeling real nice

Waves chase the sand

And sun chases moon

My lips chase your lips

Hips shake, I swoon.

I want one… do you mind?

Feels unreal, got me feeling real high

Birds have their nests

Bees have their hive

I want your kiss to be mine, never goodbye.

Linger Longer

THE BLACK PEN

You fill up my space with God when you do that

Don't you dare stop doing that… yeah, keep doing that

…looking at me like that… smiling at me like that

See, I know you gotta go and I know you just don't know

I mean, you want to hold on but this ain't how you flow

But, you and me, we flow, so please don't run cold

'Cus your arms feel a lot like home

And, suddenly I don't feel so alone

So, even though they "nose" and this ain't how you roll

I know you feel it in your bones like, the heartbeat of a song

And, we're not supposed to want more, but, I still can't help but hope

So, if you know what I know… and I know that it is so

No rush love, we can slow…

Please… just a lil bit mo"

Linger longer love, don't go.

Where Love Walks

THE BLACK PEN

I want to rest my heart where love sleeps
Peacefully and quietly, wrapped in satin sheets
I want to breathe the air that love breathes
Inhaling and exhaling the sweetness of sour dreams

Take me to the waterfall where love takes its leaps
To the place behind man's eye where secrets seldom creep
The depth of ancient souls within the realm of ice and fire
Somewhere in the darkness where four longing hands meet

I want to walk the path where love walks
Barefoot clay dances and midnight porch talks
I want to live my life as freely as the soaring hawks
Devoted to this land where every tear begets green stalks

Take me to the river where love was baptized
To the home of my forefathers and their many loving wives
The vastness of blue oceans where the lonely are cast away
Some place undiscovered where youth beget the wise

I want to grow old where love lives
Rocking on oak floors with sacred wisdom to give
I want to hum the lullaby that love sweetly sings
Fanning away the flies in spring, daydreaming of my wings

Take me to the waterfall where love takes its leaps
To the place behind your brown eyes where dreams never catch their z's
You are the silver lining, whoever you may be
Walk the path, breathe the breath that leads your soul to me.

The Space We Share

THE BLACK PEN

Deep soul reflecting desire and compassion

Observer of my existence... chatters of laughter

Short days and long nights, we exchange vowels

Gentle rough hands caressing my hips

As though they were created to fit right there

Right now...

Here.

Hopeful eyes shining like coals of amber

Luscious lips curving upward, teasing, inviting

As the tainted purity of the tongue says that

We are worthy, I am. And we are where we should be

The same...

Here.

Four legs tied together like ribbon

Wrapped around every precious piece of scenery

Shoulder kisses and childlike giggles

As feet play hide n seek underneath white cotton sheets

Here.

Sweet sighing of reminiscence and foretelling

Thumb wars and tic tac toe exchanges

We keep time from leaving us behind

Here.

Strong fingers walking beneath lacey bridges

They search for and find honey hives

THE BLACK PEN

Here.

You and I creating monuments

Here.

Beautiful memories

Here.

Epic Love

Here.

Epic Black Love

Here...

Here in the space we share.

Ignite Me

THE BLACK PEN

The dance 'tween our thoughts...

Like electric fire, burns

Possibilities...

    Sparks like this ain't real

    Yet, I see you, hear... smell you.

    Sparks like us are real.

        You speak, I listen

        So, tell me something good, love.

        "It's your soul. It's you"

            Let's go out tonight

            Pizza and wine if you please

            Life can be so nice

                Let's fall in love, luv

                Grow up, glow up, let's leap, love

                Don't be afraid, love.

                    Are you ready now?

                    You ready to hold me now?

                    Although black eyes see?

I too, dream a kiss

Of your brown honey dipped lips

Kiss me! If you dare.

    You ignite me, King

    Wanting burns within my soul

    You, "Holy Ghost Fire" me.

        Write out this love song

        Sing it til your tongue turns blue

        Manifest this truth.

Intimacy

THE BLACK PEN

My black skin against your black skin

Against mine on yours

In yours, in mine

And yours is mine, for a time.

The pause of it all... the still stance

Love still standing... still dancing... still black

And bare and raw and beautiful... you.

I sculpt your majestic silhouette with my mind

Undressing me first with your eyes

Explosions and eruptions

Uncertainties and questions never asked

As we bask in the possibility of the purity of you

Flowing into me... gently

Roughly... deeply... like oceans

That have yet to be explored... Yemoja untamed

After dark... into the dawn as we lay

Awake and existing within pleasure

Just for the sake of forsaking not

Love, this is, not soul ties, but life.

I watch ocean waves spritz from your forehead

To your face...to your neck and down your chest

Imagining the taste of the place where your true crown rests, King.

I could go on like this for hours... days...

Moments after more moments

Being consumed by you

Dreaming of my black skin against your black skin

Against mine, on yours... which is mine and ours

In my mind.

Tall, Dark & Delicious

THE BLACK PEN

Every dark desire is in his walk.
He moves like he's hunting..
Intentional, masterful, all knowing... all seeing.
I watch him with ease knowing he'd never hunt me
He'd never hurt me. Even if he doesn't know it yet.
He doesn't need to hunt me... he need only ask
And I come... I always cum for him.
He is ancient, like the tallest trees in the rainforest...
Holding the memory of lives long gone within his pores.
His beauty is unmatched... untouched... untamed
He is the definition of awe.
His laughter causes earthquakes and tidal waves
It is robust and powerful... deep;
like hidden coves at the ocean's floor.
You don't fall for a man like him...
No, you walk willingly into captivity, begging to stay.
I am enslaved by his excellence,
Captivated by his fear and sanely in love with his hope...
His vision... His dreams... His infinite possibilities.
He has a gleam in his dark eyes that says
"Life is a fairytale"
He knows it's not, but something in him finds beauty in it all.
I find beauty in it all... through his eyes.
His life is a gift, not for him but for me...
For everyone, like me, who sees who he truly is.
He is a prayer, a poem, a love story, a fight
I just want to cuddle up inside of him...
Somewhere within the core of him and stay there,
Listening to his heart beats and soul cries.
Listening to the hunger in his belly screaming out for justice.
He is a sight, a sound, a feeling to behold.
If the world needed to know what a man was like here,
They'd only need to look at him... study him.
To me, he is every man. What a man should be.
Tall, Dark and Delicious...
He is...Everything.

Black

Life

Soft Spaces

THE BLACK PEN

I wander into lit up places
Bare feet and naked flesh
I wind my hips in silence
Waist beads and crystal niplets
I hum a midnight song
Like the nightingale outside
I wash my soul in tears and sweat
The cleansing of the pride
This softness is my sanctuary
My feminine unleashed
This soft space is my love song
My freedom, my majesty.

THE BLACK PEN

I need air so fresh that I can taste the buzz of honeybees on the breeze

I need water so pure that I can taste my own reflection as it drips from my lips

I need fire so hot, that it purifies and ignites the core of my existence

I need Earth so raw that it vibrates with me; with the swing of my hips.

Give me the sacred rhythm of your drumming heart

The sound of ancestors worshiping at dusk

The feeling of sweet sweat dripping down my back beneath the sun's gaze

The feeling of copper ankhs and cowrie shells tickling my flesh

The feeling of burning sage, cinnamon brooms, and candlelight

I want to feel life so alive that each breath is a praise dance

I need water… pure water… where every tear springs a river

And every ocean is a pathway to freedom and infinite fulfillment of dreams

I need to feel that heat! I need to feel Jesus and Shango

I need to feel the embrace of Mother Mary and of Yemoja

Baptize me in curry, Crucify me with lemon balm…

Save me with cracked conch and salted fish, rebirth me

Give me air! Give me the caramel salted sea breeze of orange spiced

I need to feel every breath and every thumping of a thriving soul

I need to taste every grain of salt from bloodied lips of dancehall brawls

To the sweet heat of red peppers and sugar lingering from a kiss

I want to live! I want to be! I want… no, I need air!

Give me your bare feet dirty dances

Grant me your dashikis and wooden bangles

Woven baskets and mango fruits

Give me freedom cries and booty rubs

Give me summer braids and baselines

Give me the pleasure of childbirth and the pain of love making

Give me your dance, Give me your song

Give me hip hop and black beauties in tutus

Give me corner stores, 40s, bongs and redemption songs

THE BLACK PEN

But mostly, just give me air

Air so fresh that I can smell the buzz of honeybees on the breeze

Honey so pure that it drips from my soul flower seed

Let me be... damn! Let me breathe.

Pride

THE BLACK PEN

Hear the roots of the Earth's children
We are growing stronger
Painted faces... enchanted eyes
Rejoicing celebrations of existence
We are here!
Raw skin stomping on wet red soil
The rains have come again
Sycamore seances at dawn
Shouting Hallelujahs with a roaring chorus
The natural bliss of being
We are here and we are free.
Lavender orange skies petition our awe
How excellent it is to be alive
We have come together to recall her greatness
Goddess! God! Mother! Liberty!
We are here! We are free! And we are chosen!
Let the laughter of our chaos reign over normal peace
Let the beauty of the unknown sting many irises
While the dullness of knowing fades deeply into abyss
It is our duty to be alive and live happily
Juniper gallops onto turquoise shores
It is our calling indeed to live in eternal joy
Pine mists and mountain songs
Shackles have been unchained
Chains have been loosed
Nooses have been cut down
We gather freely in evergreen fern valleys
We are here! We are free! We are chosen! We are inevitable!
Forests born of desert lands
The remnants of shadowed pasts
We can not be broken and refuse to be ignored
Instead, we celebrate black and brown hues
Our mahogany, cedar, and cherry tones
Can you hear that? Can you hear us?
The roots of the Earth's children ...
We are growing, we are here, we are free.

In Love With Being Black

THE BLACK PEN

My knotti hair looks good on me

Warms my head and protects my crown

Offers softness to rest on

My round nose fits perfectly on me

I can smell mommas homemade a mile away

I can smell a lie from even farther

My high cheeks sit good on me

Even when I'm frowning, I wear a constant smile

They say I look important

(side note, I am.)

My wide hips sway nicely on me

When I walk I look like I'm dancing

And when I push, it comes easily... naturally

My brownie brown skin glows sexy on me

I absorb the sun without pain or burns

I sparkle in darkness like glitter in moonlight

My infamous attitude works nicely for me

I don't take no mess! Won't take yours either

I will love you to life and fight for mine to the death

My laughter sounds damn good to me

Loud and bubbly and from the gut

It's like music to my children, its healing after all

My yoni feels real good to me

It's the essence of every man's fantasy

Its sacred, its divinity… the portal of all things wonderful

(side note, I am wonderful)

      I'm in love with myself

I'm in love with my naps, kinks, knots and curls

My smile, my nose

I love the scent of me

The taste of me

The glow of me

The high of me

I love the way I move and

I love the way the Earth moves me

I was born with God in my womb and the Earth in my chest

THE BLACK PEN

The sun in my soul and the moon in my hands

The ocean in my tears and the desert in my steps

The forest in my breath and mountains in my eyes

I'm so in love with myself

I'm in love with being worthy

I'm in love with being this damn fly

I'm in love with being black like this

...as dark... as beautiful... as black as I.

Step Queen, Step!

THE BLACK PEN

Woo wee!
That girl know she can step
Slappin' her thigh meat
Stompin those tiny feet
Rolling her neck
And droppin it low
Clappin' her hands
Watch those arms go
She creates that rhythm
She creates that vibe
All eyes are on her
She be movin, I ain't lyin
Woo wee!
That girl know she's a beast
Head high, confidence on
With her whole body, she preach
Snappin her fingers
Switchin her hips
Flippin her ponytail
And poppin her lips
Rollin her neck and droppin it low
Knees up high
And then windin' it slow
Woo wee
That girl know she can move
Got the whole crowd thumpin
All caught up in the groove
Slidin to the left
Jumpin to the right
Foot stompin the baseline
Under the spotlight
Slap, clap, snap it out
Yes, Queen Go!
Steps seem like step dreams
"Step Team?!"
"You Know!"

Bull City Bad

THE BLACK PEN

He called me a Durhamite

Like some sorta infestation

"boy who you think you talkin to"?

Rolled neck, rolled eyes... here's your education...

We be bull city strong ova here bruh

Trust, you don't want these problems

I've got goons who've got goons

Who'd love to help me solve 'em

We be thick butts and slim waists

We be Eagles, Blue Devils and screw-faced

We snap fingers and share hands, we supply and we demand

Knuckin bucks while sangin Amazing Grace

We eat Churches and Bojangles

Cook Out shakes and Chicken Hut

La Maracas on Tuesdays

House parties and southern guts

Did he call me Durhamite?

Like some sorta insult?

Boy bye! I proudly bump my fists together

Horns up, thumbs out, black power nympho

Sloping hills and history

Black wall street and mysteries

The Know BookStore and those jerk wings..?

Damn! These streets were good to me

Open mics at Broad Street on Thursdays

Karaoke at Carolina Ale on Wednesdays

9th Street kept it Cosmic on Fridays

Before the big "G" turned us sideways

Fancier places with foreign menus

Sure miss the good ole days

Back when the Dog House had the best cheese fries

And Duke Villa was considered classy

Hanging in the arcade at South Square Mall

Overdressed, underaged and flashy.

He called me a Durhamite

Like something to be ashamed of

Though they've replaced our spots with martini shakers

We Bull City Bad, A little hood a lotta class

A lotta pride, we black history makers.

The Yard

THE BLACK PEN

It's like magic in the summertime

Young cocoa gods high rising the scene

Young queens and kings too high up to see

Their golden dipped honey browns

Almond and caramel

Afros, plaits, twists and braids

Boxed, chopped, waves and fades

Welcome to black town.

Hear the base through the cars

They ride slow with windows down

Young future lawyers and nail shop owners

Walkin... nah, struttin around.

It's like magic in the summertime

Wrap around sandals, philosophy and tanks

Booty shorts, scandals history of black banks

Early mornings and later nights

Study sessions of life

Bantu knots, cornrows, shaves

Two-strand-twist outs, gels and pomades

Turn on the black lights.

Feel the thump through the walls

Smell the after-hours in the air

Young future fathers and mothers and dem

Whew chile! You should've been there.

It's like magic in the summertime

Young cocoa gods living in light beams

Young ones fulfilling ancestral dreams

Their bronze crowns high, their minds so free

Grants, loans and scholarships

Perms, blow-outs and sew-ins

Wigs, crochets, kinky curled lullabies

Welcome to the yard, young kings.

Hair Washing Day

THE BLACK PEN

Deep breath

Ready?

Spray bottle

Wide toothed

Towel...

Indian style

For a while...

Butt sore...

Rocking...

Switch it up.

Part, spray, comb

Part, spray, comb

And so on and so on

Clean the kitchen sink

Shake shake shake

Squeeze

Massage

Scratch it out

Pull...

Repeat…

Ahhh! My eye…

Damnit!

Towel…

Crashing into…

Something hit the floor

Something hit my foot

Where's that towel?

Water on

Towel soaked

"keke! Bring me a towel"

Rinse. Repeat.

Deep Condition.

Hot oil.

Wipe red eyes.

Water everywhere.

Other towel found.

Clean the kitchen sink.

Mop the floor.

THE BLACK PEN

Feet up. Hour up.

Water on. Rinse. Repeat.

Wring it out.

Part.

Coconut

Tea tree

Shea

Leave-in

Part, comb, apply, repeat.

Plait.

Rest arms.

Plait some more.

'Til done...

Now done.

Air dry.

Damn! I'm tired...

I'm bout to get braids.

More
(An ode to black women)

THE BLACK PEN

I am more than my phat ass and waistline

I am more than my full lips and kinky hair

I am more than my high cheek bones

But I understand the confusion...

See, I know that beauty didn't have a name until there was me

I know that the Earth didn't have formation

Until my womb birthed it out

I know that when the sun shines on me, I become a prism...

Every color dancing within my melanin drip.

Its overwhelming, I know, to be in my presence

And for the weak of heart, its easy to get lost in the shell

But I am a divine being... a divine goddess... not an appearance

Not an attitude, not a problem, not a baby momma but a queen

I am the queen mother of every nation

I have given birth to planets, many moons and every star

I have crouched low in valleys, my birthing fluid, creating your rivers and streams

My salty tears and sweat have given you oceans

I have laughed such full laughs that the sky thundered

I have danced such wild dances that new lands were formed at my feet

But, you see me and forget who the fuck you're taking to...

Who the hell do you think you're talking to?

"yo ma"? "aye yo bitch"? "thot"? "cunt"? "hoe"?

Young man! Have you lost your damn mind?

"let me smack that"? "you cute for a dark skinned…"?

Boy child, what would your grandmother say?

What would your ancestors say?

If you think you have the balls to speak to me…

Be sure they're big enough to approach me correctly

Queen, Love, Light, Goddess, Mother, Wife, Divinity, Infinity…

that's me.

See, I am more than my phat ass and waistline

I am more than the nut that you wish you could get

I am more than my swaying hips and chocolate skin

I am your inspiration, your driving force, your why, your reason

I am your auntie, your daughter, your grandmother, your mother

I am your teacher and favorite student… I'm your neighbor, your bus driver

I am your congresswoman, your Vice President, your doctor and your lawyer

I nursed you, bathed you, clothed you, fed you…

Nigga I created you!

So, however overwhelmed and ignorant you may be

Whatever silly title you've placed over me…

However tight your pants may be whenever you see me…

Of all the goodness and beauty in this world…

I was, I am and will always be…

More.

The Hungry

THE BLACK PEN

Feed me

Feed me

Feed me

Hear the silent cries of the shattered

Starving for the salvation from your tongue

Speak up! Speak out! Reach out for us...

The Neo! A Christ. The One.

Mickey Dees is phony

Taco Tuesday leaves us sick

Give us that grandma's homemade love

Made with blood, sweat and breast milk

We need something to bite into

Our senses crave something raw

Cook it up for us, yes take your time

Your spit manifesting new Law.

Give us this day our daily bread

Preach us this day our truth

Freedom ringing loud and strong

From the bosom of Sister Ruth

This ain't a meal to tear into

No, this one requires time

Savoring every adjective

Butter creams lubricating the mind

This is no simple task Chef Light

Revealing the hidden and forgotten

Raining mana in this desert land

2 loaves, 5 fish, a milk carton

Feed us! Hear the children cry

Like its early on Thanksgiving Eve

Chop it up, slice it and serve it up now

Nourishment that souls do need.

Hungry eyes are holding out hands

A little mac, A little roast, A little cheese

Hear the desperate cries of homeless eyes

Feed us!

Feed us!

Feed me.

All Hail The Black Pen

THE BLACK PEN

You tell the story oh so well

Yes, you tell the story

Men and women lost and proud

The struggle and the glory

Man do they listen when you open up your heart

You pour our pain out like molasses on pages,

dripping from your fingertips

Making us move and remember, cry and remember

Oh how we remember... like dancing in September

Like James' foot work and Michael's howl

Your words remind us to do better, to be better right now

Man I know that pen's getting heavier and heavier

While the unashamed **black** faced listeners

are getting deadlier and deadlier

You arm us with wisdom and power... **black** power

You spark up our hearts like fireworks that light up **black** eyes in July

Making us want to stand taller... hold our heads higher

Oh, how our fist go higher...Crushing the façade of white liars

In their white cotton sheets... burning crosses at cross streets

Your tongue reminds us to be proud of the **black** souls freed

Man you know these **black** minds getting freer and freer

While the ones with long lines of bleached bread

getting greedier and greedier

But we ready now... ready to stand up now

Oh child, got that knowledge and power now

Remember when they tried to break us all the way down?

Yeah, you reminded us of that

...wouldn't let us forget none of that...

So many of trying to make it, we started forgetting about that **black**

Bout those bruises and scars hidden on grandmother's back...

THE BLACK PEN

But now you've got us marching on pages... got our souls clapping back.

You shole do yell the story well

Man, I swear you tell the story

Black faces fighting for the right to be

Black pride! **Black** power! **Black** glory!

In loving memory of:
*Mariam Lee,
Tiara Tyler,
Shamel Brailsford,
and Shaun Bagley*

In honor of:
*Robert B. Miller
(Black Superman)*

LaDonna Letitia has been writing since she first learned her ABC's. With a Language Arts teacher for a mother and mentors like Maya Angelou, Billie Holiday and Octavia Butler, her love for words is what pushed her through the various challenges of living as a POC in the states.

Although Science Fiction is her greatest love, she has entered into the publishing world as a rising powerhouse in poetry and writing as a whole. Her first work, "the BLACK pen" is just a glimpse of what the public has to look forward to in the future.

As a dancer, a lyricist, a poet, a mentor, an activist, a creative and light worker, LaDonna strives to create safe spaces within the pages of her writing where people of color can let go and be att-one-ment with themselves.

She continues to study life and create in ALL forms and is currently working on a collection of Sci-Fi short stories.